O9-AIG-620

CHRISTMAS IN IRELAND

CHRISTMAS IN IRELAND

Introduced

by

COLIN MORRISON

in association with

THE MERCIER PRESS

The Mercier Press
4 Bridge Street, Cork, &
24 Lower Abbey Street, Dublin 1.

© The Contributors, 1989

First Published 1989
Reprinted 1990

British Library Cataloguing in Publication Data
Christmas in Ireland.
   1. English Literature. Irish writers, to 1985
   Special subjects: Christmas — Anthologies
   820.8'033

   ISBN 0-85342-950-2

Christmas in Ireland is based on the RTE 1 Radio programme
'Cast Your Mind to Bethlehem' produced by Colin Morrison.

'An Ulster Twilight' from STATION ISLAND by Seamus Heaney.
Copyright © 1985 by Seamus Heaney.
Reprinted by permission of Farrar, Straus and Giroux, Inc.

Typeset in Garamond by
Seton Music Graphics Ltd, Bantry, Co. Cork.
Printed in Ireland by Colour Books Ltd., Dublin.

CONTENTS

Introduction

COLIN MORRISON

I nicked six nicks on the door-post
With my penknife's big blade —
There was a little one for cutting tobacco.
And I was six Christmases of age . . .

. . .

My father played the melodeon,
My mother milked the cows,
And I had a prayer like a white rose pinned
On the Virgin Mary's blouse.

Patrick Kavanagh

Christmas time in the Irish landscape has not only deeply moved and inspired Patrick Kavanagh to greatness on numerous occasions, but also Yeats, Joyce, O'Casey and Heaney, the list is endless — and why should it not be so? We are all in our own way indelibly imprinted with memories of different shades, colours and intensities of those early Christmases in our lives. Days of expectations, fulfilled and unfulfilled — relations familiar and forgotten.

I can still see in my mind's eye, on Christmas Eve in my early childhood, my father and myself kneeling at his bedroom window looking south from Clontarf across the darkening skyscape of Dublin Bay to the Pigeon House and then beyond to Dun Laoghaire, Dalkey, the Mugglins and finally eastwards towards the Kish Lighthouse — we scanned the Christmas sky, for what seeemed like hours for a sight of Santa Claus, reindeers and sleigh.

'But where will he land?'

'Over our garden wall, on the tennis courts in the church grounds.'

St John's Church of Ireland, where unseen then as now on Christmas Eve the lonely doers of the parish dress altar, nave, transcept and porch in their Christmas best for both saints and sinners to meet their personal God on Christmas morn — that same God we all uneasily carry around in our souls. St John's Church of Ireland Church, whose spire on bright summer days as young exhausted tennis players we would lie under on our backs in the damp grass, watching the clouds rushing on their way to who knows where over the rusted ever facing north weather cock — and thanks to an illusion of nature, we would wait for the toppling tower to crush us all the way to the gates of eternity — maybe it would fall on the rectory — when the rector and his family were out of course, and split the dark victorian structure in two — then what fun we'd have!

'How will Santa Claus know where we are?'

8

'Does he have a map?'

'What will we do if he crashes, what then?'

'What if Eric Robinson sees him first?'

Questions, questions, questions — the answers patiently given and never doubted.

Do we like Kavanagh weave around our memories of Christmas a romantic cloak, and if we do, why not? What memories will this Christmas Eve unfold? Maybe, the dim picture of my mother on the days approaching Christmas, sitting on the sofa by the fire — me at her feet, watching her patiently wrap and label the season's presents. How I envied her copper-plated hand-writing. Would I ever be able to emulate her distinctive style? Time has proved not.

Her passion for music meant at Christmas, the blending of Oratorio, Hymn and Carol, in what seemed like every corner of the house, that, punctuated with stories weaved from her Christmases before 'The Rebellion'. Tales of stiff-collared relations, moulded in Victorian Ireland, stiff-collared only on the surface, and children being children, 'thank God', despite the expec-tations of the elders. My mother loved every moment of that unexplained atmosphere unique to Christmas, that strikes, if we are lucky to our very core — and so unashamedly do I. So when some years ago, I was asked to produce and compile a radio programme, to be broadcast on the night before Christmas, I asked our distinguished programme contributors, to unearth and reflect in prose, poetry, and music their townland through their Christmas memories. The result can now be enjoyed between these covers. They will, I hope entertain and move the reader to the point where the seasonal gift will abound.

Like this my memory saw
Like this my childhood heard
These pilgrims of the North.
And memory, you have me spared
A light to follow them
Who go to Bethlehem.

Patrick Kavanagh

COLIN MORRISON 1989

Quotations from the poems of Patrick Kavanagh are used by permission of the Trustees of Patrick Kavanagh, c/o Peter Fallon, Literary Agent, Loughcrew, Oldcastle, County Meath.

Many Years Ago

JOHN B. KEANE

Many years ago, in our street, there lived an old woman who had but one son who's name was Jack. Jack's father had died when Jack was no more than a gorsoon but Jack's mother went out to work to support her son and herself.

As Jack grew older she still went out and worked for the good reason that Jack did not like work. The people in the street used to say that Jack was only good for three things. He was good for eating, he was good for smoking and he was good for drinking. Now to give him his due he never beat his mother or abused her verbally. All he did was to skedaddle to England when she was too old to go out to work. Years passed but she never had a line from her only son. Every Christmas she would stand inside her window waiting for a card or a letter. She waited in vain.

When Christmas came to our street it came with a loud laugh and an expansive humour that healed old wounds and lifted the hearts of young and old. If the Christmas that came to our street were a person he would be something like this: he would be in his

11

sixties but glowing with rude health. His face would be flushed and chubby with sideburns down to the rims of his jaws. He would be wearing gaiters and a tweed suit and he would be mildly intoxicated. His pockets would be filled with silver coins for small boys and girls and for the older folk he would have a party at which he would preside with his waistcoated paunch, extending benignly, and his posterior benefiting from the glow of a roaring log fire.

There would be scalding punch for everybody and there would be roast geese and ducks, their beautiful golden symmetries exposed in large dishes and tantalising gobs of potato-stuffing oozing and bursting from their rear-end stitches. There would be singing and storytelling and laughter and perhaps a tear here and there when absent friends were toasted. There would be gifts for everybody and there would be great good will, as neighbours embraced, promising to cherish each other till another twelve months had passed.

But you see Christmas is an occasion and not a person. A person can do things, change things, create things but all our occasions are only what we want them to be. For this reason Jack's mother waited Christmas after Christmas for word of her wandering boy. To other houses would come stout, registered envelopes from distant loved ones who remembered. There would be bristling, crumply envelopes from America with noble rectangular cheques to delight the eye and comfort the soul. There would be parcels and packages of all shapes and sizes so that every house became a warehouse until the great day came when all goods would be distributed.

Now it happened that in our street there was a postman who knew a lot more about his residents than they knew about themselves. When Christmas came he was weighted with bags of letters and parcels. People awaited his arrival the way children awaited a bishop on confirmation day. He was not averse to indulging in a drop of the comforts wherever such comforts were tendered but comforts or no comforts the man was always sensitive to the need of others. In his heart resided the spirit of Christmas. Whenever he came to the house where the old woman lived he would crawl on all fours past the window. He just didn't have the heart to go by and be seen by her. He hated to disappoint people, particularly old people. For the whole week before Christmas she would take up her position behind the faded curtains, waiting for the letter which never came.

Finally the postman could bear it no longer. On Christmas Eve he delivered to our house a mixed bunch of cards and letters. Some were from England. He requested one of these envelopes when its contents were removed. He re-wrote the name and address and also he wrote a short note which he signed 'your loving son Jack'. Then from his pocket he extracted a ten shilling note, a considerable sum in those far off days. He placed the note in the envelope. There was no fear the old woman would

13

notice the handwriting because if Jack was good at some things, as I have already mentioned, he was not good at other things at all and one of these was writing. In fact Jack could not write his own name. When the postman came to the old woman's door he knocked loudly. When she appeared he put on his best official voice and said 'sign for this if you please Missus'. The old woman signed and opened the envelope. The tears appeared in her eyes and she cried out loud: 'I declare to God but Jack is a scholar'.

'True for you,' said the postman, 'and I daresay he couldn't get in touch with you until he learned to write.'

'I always knew there was good in him,' she said. 'I always knew it.'

'There's good in everyone Missus,' said the postman, as he moved on to the next house.

The street was not slow in getting the message and in the next and last post there were many parcels for the old woman. It was probably the best Christmas the street ever had.

Dangling

MICHEAL O'SIADHAIL

Unstrapped from the car-roof, brushed
past our halldoor jamb, it shed
its first needles. We rushed, fetched
cones with silvered scales, striped
lanterns, painted globes, crackers,
tokens of magic hurriedly dangled
by a thread. The tallest fastened
a star to its peak, draped over
its branches a hoarfrost of tinsel.
An infinite festivity still stretched
ahead as we dressed green with gaiety.

In a glisten of excitement, when fairy
lights shone coloured kisses
blown in the dark, one night
I slipped alone into the cold street.
I don't remember why — maybe
to see the glow in the window, to peep
at childhood's warmth from without.

Now on forest walks, humble
against the silence of huge
spruces, I gaze at light trembling
in their spires, pause to shake
away a veil of dew. To assuage
winter's disbelief I need to touch
those twigs, feel green pledges
that March decks out the birch
with a new lingerie of leaf,
that spring won't stand us up,
or leave this lover in the lurch.

Christmas For Us Small Lads

EAMON KELLY

Christmas for us small lads growing up in the 1920s was a pool of light in the inky darkness of winter. A soft amber pool of warm light which came from three sources – the big log and turf fire, the oil lamp with the hair-pin straddling the glass chimney and the stately white candles, one in every window, spreading their light out into the yard and road showing the way, the old people told us, to Joseph and Mary should they be passing in search of shelter on Christmas night. Although my father used to say that if they happened to be passing our house the blessed pair would have strayed a tidy step from the road to Bethlehem.

In the month of December there was no road darker than the road outside our house, for we were living in the depths of the country, and as yet the ESB poles hadn't come marching down the valley bringing with them a brighter but a harsher light. And it cuts me to the quick today when I hear that instead of the old tallow candle there is a new garish, electric imitation lighting in many of the windows I looked on as a lad.

It was the quality of the candlelight, too shy you'd say to penetrate into every nook and corner, and giving the kitchen the appearance of an old oil painting that I remember best about Christmases long ago. I remember too all the work that went into making the house ready for the feast — bringing in the berry holly to deck out the kitchen, fixing the candles and cutting the log, bloc na Nollag, and placing it in position on the hearth lying flat as it fell we were told and the sods of turf standing as they were cut. It took the block some time to take fire but when it did the chairs had to be moved back, even the cat shifted herself when little jets of steam and sparks making loud reports came from the log. In the wider circle we, the smaller lads, sat on the floor with cups of lemonade and sweet cake after the Christmas Eve supper of ling, white onion sauce and laughing potatoes. And we made room for a neighbour or two while my father uncorked the big earthenware jar and landed out a few healthy taoscáns of the dark liquid and it was 'Merry Christmas, Happy Christmas everyone,' re-echoing what was painted on the mottoes pinned to the chimney breast.

The hearth was the friendliest place in the house. The place to talk, to sing, to listen to a good story, to hear the conversation of the grown ups and let on not to hear the bits of gossip or some scandal our elders seemed to take an unlaughing pleasure in. The hearth was the place where the mother read out the American letters from Aunt Margaret, Aunt Mary and

18

our Aunt Bridgie and counted out the dollars, they, and Aunty Liz, had sent to us. We would all repeat the American address where our Aunts lived to see who'd remember it best. It was Ditmaar's Boulevard, Astoria, Queens, Long Island, New York, New York. The hearth was the place where we knelt before the supper on Christmas Eve for the rosary with the trimmings we thought would never end.

When it was time for us small lads to go to bed we'd hang up our stockings along the mantle shelf and on the crane to make sure Daidí na Nollag wouldn't forget us. Even if it was only a new penny it would be welcome. A penny was a great treat at the time when you would get five bull's eyes for a ha'penny and two peggy's legs for a full penny. In the end we would have to be hunted to bed we would be so lazy leaving the warm hearth, but the promise of driving in the pony and trap through the dark for early Mass in the morning would finally shift us, but we weren't gone yet. We'd all have to stand at the front door for a while admiring the bunches of lights in the houses down along the valley and up the rising ground to Rossacrew; all the little lights winking and blinking through the dark until, as the man said, the earth below seemed like a reflection of the starry heavens above.

The Age-Old Message

PAT INGOLDSBY

And the age-old message of Christmas moves quietly from the stable. A baby cries and his mother looks love. Cow's breath mists and clouds on sharp frosty air. Wrap the infant warm and snug and gently place him in the waiting straw. Sing 'Gloria in Excelsis Deo' across the mountains, echo it up and into the star-filled shivering skies and into the hearts of men. Hill-top shepherds know and sense and come to kneel and hold a baby lamb in strong and gentle arms for this is a gift. Peace to all men and some are far away from home, behind the high grey wall where all the doors are locked and a cell is as lonely as a stable when all of your family is many miles away and you are further still.

Tonight the message of Christmas lives and loves for all people and moves quietly over the grey walls and in through locked doors and says, 'Tonight we are a family for unto everyone of us a child is born, whoever and wherever you are on this most sacred of nights.'

Do not pull any more triggers. Let the guns be stilled forever. Place your weapons on the ground and walk away from them. Tonight is made for you and your brothers and sisters and tonight you belong . . . together. The night air is still and trembling with the message. Do not fill it with the alien sound of gunfire. Open up your heart instead and if you must hold a gun, only hold it for as long as it takes you to place it on the ground and walk away from it.

Listen . . . voices are singing and the words are specially for you and your brothers and sisters. All is calm . . . all is quiet. Listen to the words and hear them. A message for all mankind and some are not going home tonight. A girl in white moves silently between rows of sleeping beds, moving on tip-toe and hearing the voices of men who talk and mutter in their sleep. They call her 'Nurse' and they have a special way of saying it. 'Nurse' is nineteen and many of them are father-age and look and laugh and talk with the girl who could be daughter. She is nineteen and now she sees them sleeping for tonight she is keeping watch while men of father-age are far away in sleep.

The children are sleeping too . . . eyes tight shut for fear that they might waken and see . . . don't look . . . mustn't look . . . Santa knows. The children are sleeping warm and safe and adventure-dreaming snow-filled, present-wrapped, Santa-laughing, silver-tinselled, robin red-breasted dreams that tumble headlong towards the early morning gallop down the stairs and 'Look look . . . oh look what he brought me!'

Airport-crowded, scarf-muffled, suitcase-crammed and boarding at gate 14. All good children go to sleep

21

and we are going home. A long time away in a strange land and home is warm at Christmas and the lights are never so welcome as when you see them from a long time, long way off.

Garda slow slow measured steps, checking doorways, thinking home and holly thoughts, torch shining into shadow dark archways, doorways, porches. Once upon a long time ago he wore a gun and holster cowboy suit on Christmas morning. Now he slow slow steps his lonely late-night vigil. Young man in a garda suit looks towards the sky and knows and senses and smiles. Candles window-flicker gold and welcome for mother who was homeless and with child and every door was closed and no room was anywhere and now the candles flicker gold and say, 'We love you – you are welcome.'

Do not be afraid tonight. Come and adore him instead. Kneel with every creed and every colour and all are one. For unto us a child is born and unto everyone . . . young asleep, old alone, prison-celled, hospital-bound, come and adore him in your own way and in your own words and take your place in the family where there is a place for everyone and money will never be the measure of a man when all are quiet and all are still and listening to the words of the message. Even now it is moving gently into hearts which are open on this most wondrous of nights. The words are good and the words are true and the words are forever. Peace on earth, goodwill to all men.

An Ulster Twilight

SEAMUS HEANEY

The bare bulb, a scatter of nails,
Shelved timber, glinting chisels:
In a shed of corrugated iron
Eric Dawson stoops to his plane

At five o'clock on a Christmas Eve.
Carpenter's pencil next, the spoke-shave,
Fretsaw, auger, rasp and awl,
A rub with a rag of linseed oil.

A mile away it was taking shape,
The hulk of a toy battleship,
As waterbuckets iced and frost
Hardened the quiet on roof and post.

Eric Dawson, where are you now?
There were fifteen years between us two
That night I strained to hear the bells
Of a sleigh of the mind and heard him pedal

Into our lane, get off at the gable,
Steady his Raleigh bicycle
Against the whitewash, stand to make sure
The house was quiet, knock at the door

And hand his parcel to a peering woman:
'I suppose you thought I was never coming.'
Eric, tonight I saw it all
Like shadows on your workshop wall,

Smelled wood shavings under the bench,
Weighed the cold steel monkey-wrench
In my soft hand, then stood at the road
To watch your wavering tail-light fade

And knew that if we met again
In an Ulster twilight we would begin
And end whatever we might say
In a speech all toys and carpentry,

A doorstep courtesy to shun
Your father's uniform and gun,
But – now that I have said it out –
Maybe none the worse for that.

Reprinted by permission of Faber and Faber Ltd from Station Island *by Seamus Heaney.*

Christmas Time Machine

HUGH LEONARD

It was Marcel Proust who said: 'The true paradises are the paradises we have lost'. In his great work, *A La Recherche du temps perdu,* the narrator is carried back to the past by tasting a cake — a Madeleine it is called, dipped in tea. I have my own kind of time machine, and all I have to do to set it in motion is polish my shoes. They have to be black shoes, because my father's boots were black and I no sooner begin to dab on the polish, when I see him on Christmas Eve, bringing those Sunday boots of his to a shine so dazzling, that in it you could see the room and all it contained.

I begin to see other things in the room, the images like an iris opening out as when a scene begins in a silent film. My mother is stuffing the turkey, I am sitting in a corner, my nose in a book. I pretend to be reading it, but instead I am holding my breath, waiting for Christmas to happen. The kitchen is somehow unfamiliar, it gleams. The range has been black-leaded, the china dogs polished, the lid on the iron kettle is almost leaping from the heat of the fire, the decorations are up, long paper chains, swooping from the four corners of the room, and rising again to meet in the middle above the single light bulb with the dusty shade. There's holly behind every picture, even the holy ones. And I know that tomorrow, the Room will be in use, I wish I could pronounce it as I write it, with a capital R. It was pressed into services for great occasions, First Communions, or Confirmations perhaps, or a rare visit from Mrs Pim, in whose father's three and a half acre garden, my own father had worked, since he was fourteen, in 1897. And of course it was used for Christmas.

Tomorrow morning Mr Quirke from next door would come in, his hard hat scraping the lintel. 'God save all here' was his greeting 'when I get in meself', and twenty minutes later he would stoop his way out again, this time, with a fine white flavoursome froth adorning his snuff-yellowed moustache. The Room, still with the capital R, will be used again in the afternoon, when my friends would come for an hour, and stare at the unfamiliarity of the side-board, the vase of honesty and the oval pictures of the pier at Llandudno, and a fire would burn in the grate, while we ate cream biscuits and drank a half glass of Gilbey's port wine, so cloyingly sweet that you wondered how Uncle Sonny could bear to be drunk every Saturday. Nowadays when I see an old film, I often remember how I felt when I saw it as an eight-year old, half a century ago. I even remember, in whose company I was that day, and what my mother said when it was

26

over. 'Oul' codology', was her most withering verdict.

I don't think I sentimentalise when I think back on those Christmases with a sense of loss. We ate ice cream in summer then, never in winter, as we do now. We had turkey once a year, a rare and marvellous treat and not as when someone decides in April or July or September that it would make a nice change. We were poor for 364 days and when we celebrated Christmas, it was not just a religious holiday, or even a time for gluttony and life's pleasure. It was a testimony to our survival through another year. The world is different. As we watch one film on television on Christmas Day, the chances are that the video machine is working away, recording a second one on another channel. And these, make no mistake, are not wonders, for wonders happen once a year, not every day. My own family is no exception to the new way of things. We do not stint ourselves throughout the year, and so there is no newness, or sense of paradise, about Christmas. And yet I remember exactly how it was and how to get back inside the skin of that small boy again, who saw Christmas as a great necklace of diamonds, from first awakening to midnight sleep, with the sweetness of that port wine, still on his tongue. I go there along a thread of memory, and it is not a thread at all.

I look closely and see it for what it is. My father's boot lace.

And Maybe This is Christmas

PAT INGOLDSBY

You wouldn't look twice at her. One or two did glance but there just wasn't time to do anything else beyond that. People rushing, barging, pushing, rushing home. 'Get the last of the cheeky Charlies, the holly with the berries, get the last few sprigs of mistletoe'. Get a bus, a train, a lift, a Dart, put the parcels down, find the car-keys, rush, push, God is that the time, hurry on down to Heuston and clickedly Christmas clack to Kerry, Galway, Cork and don't look back or you might just turn into a . . .

You wouldn't look twice at her. One or two did glance and split-second thought about a long time far-away woman who was heavy with child and when you are heavy with parcels you can always stop and fumble for the small change all change at Limerick Junction and Mallow and it's great to see you home so don't delay now and fumble now but rush on down to Heuston and she can shuffle on.

She doesn't know that she is every woman who ever sat beneath the frozen statue and didn't raise her head to see the red and blue and green and orange bulbs' cold-glow up there in the sky-reaching spreadeagled branches.

She doesn't sit there long because the parcel-people rushing rush and the urgency reaches through horn-beeping traffic roar and slowly eases her up to move again and shuffle some place else.

She doesn't know it but she is every woman who ever limped into the church because it's warm until they lock the doors and shuffle you on out to the other side of them.

Thinking crazy holly-pricked thoughts, climb, go on, clamber, struggle over the altar rails. In there is hay and infant and cows and donkey breathing warmth until you put out your hand to steady yourself and altar rail is cold white marble cold and you are old shoebroken old.

And then she met the man on the outside of the surging rushing people. Him standing, orange shadow in the light of a million shop windows.

Him drawn towards her 'don't know where I'm going eyes' because he didn't know either. He put his arms around her and he drew her into him and she wanted to ask him — 'Are you my son?' But she was tired of asking and tired of looking so she let him hold her instead. He was tired of sleeping under cardboard and sitting under frozen statues and asking old women old enough — 'Are you my mother?' And so he held her.

They open creaked the door where it was warm and candles flicker-danced and up there on the wall,

Christ was falling three times a day for anybody who stopped three times a day to look up and see. No sound but their footsteps shuffling up to Bethlehem which was near enough to walk. Up there at the top of the wooden creaking floorboard aisle where the people would stand after midnight, close-pressed inching forward to receive His body.

He wasn't holding her now but the closeness between them made it as good and safe and warm for her as if he was. They stood together and they looked at the hay and the roof-drifting sparkling cotton-wool snow. They looked at the shepherds leaning forward and Joseph bent on one knee and the pair of them kneeling on two.

They had come to adore him because they had no place to sleep. They had come to adore him because cardboard sheets are cold and rain is sleeting wet and midnight Mass is free and afterwards you are very very hungry. They knelt for much longer than their prayers because the pipes along the walls are warm and Bethlehem behind the altar rails is where you want to be when your crazy holly-pricked thoughts are still shrieking—'Are you my son?' You are still afraid to ask because you don't know where he came from and maybe he will know where there are better than cardboard sheets and maybe you will sleep inside his arms and maybe you will sleep in heavenly peace.

And maybe this is Christmas.

Christmas Time

BREANDÁN Ó hEITHIR

For almost twenty-five years, all my Christmases were dominated by the sea that flowed between the island of Inis Mór and the mainland. No matter how early the Christmas fare was ordered on the mainland, there were certain things that could only come on the boat that sailed on Christmas Eve. The sea was always calm on Christmas Eve as I remember it, but a child always fears the worst and enjoys the fulfilment of his desires, all the more, when his fears are not realised.

Later, when Christmas meant travelling home by boat from boarding school, calm seas were also desired. Afterwards, when Little Christmas was over, the signs by which the knowledgeable forecast the weather were sought for indications of severe and prolonged south-westerly gales. On one memorable occasion, one of the great gales of my youth, stretched the Christmas holiday by a full week. It was the year of the *Flying Enterprise* and Captain Carlsen, who's adventures on the mountainous seas, south of Ireland, we followed nightly on the wireless, and later saw on the newsreels in the cinema in Galway.

And later still, when working in Dublin I was one of those inhabitants who 'went home' for Christmas. Home from Westland Row on the train, among the tall men in the blue suits, and the canary coloured pullovers, who packed the bar, waving white English ten pound notes and talking of exotic places like Swindon, Watford, Slough and Willesden. They were part of the Irish army of occupation who had pulled down what Hitler spared of the English towns and cities and were now re-building them. I remember the songs they sang and how uneasily their snatches of English slang sat on the soft accents and colourful speech of their western parishes.

Then came the year when Dublin claimed me. I met many friends, particularly, when late in the evening, I arrived in Henry Street, where the last of the jumping dolls, the Christmas lights, the fruit and the very, very last turkeys were being energetically barked. This was Radio Éireann country, and one of my friends in that institution, who definitely never 'went home' for Christmas, was standing in the door, surveying the passing scene. This was Séamus Kavanagh, actor and wit, and head of the WC department of Radio Éireann as he was fond of describing his department of Women's and Children's programmes.

We crossed the road to have a Christmas drink, and it was then we met the little man who was to cast a shadow over my first Christmas in Dublin. He caught my attention because he was drinking rum. Its vile smell was enough to expel me from any pub, ever since I had violent disagreement with a bottle of it while still a student. He was small and elderly, dressed in black, wearing a black bowler hat, and at his feet lay a large turkey, wrapped in brown paper, with only its scraggy neck and head protruding. Séamus who lived with a married sister in Aungier Street, and who was as Dublin as Liffey water, accompanied me on a short pilgrimage to the pubs of Henry Street, Mary Street, Moore Street, and we even crossed O'Connell Street at some personal risk to visit North Earl Street.

It was here we again met the little man in black. He approached us in a state of some agitation and asked: 'Didn't you two gentlemen see me in Henry Street about three hours ago?' We said that indeed we had. Somewhat cheered by this news, he held up the turkey wrapped in brown paper by its neck, and asked: 'Did I have a turkey when you saw me?'

We said that he seemed to have the same turkey that he now held in front of us by the neck.

'Ah,' said the little man, 'that's what I thought too. But it's gone you see'. And then he thrust his hand into the brown paper to show us that all that remained of the turkey was the scraggy head and neck.

Well it was Christmas and the little man was clearly in no fit state to trace the missing carcass. But after being loudly laughed out of the first four pubs we visited, Séamus had a thought. If the little man hurried, he might be in time to get another turkey in Moore Street. 'Ah,' the little man said, 'I thought of that myself, but you see, I only have the price of a few drinks and me bus fare left. I wouldn't mind, but I'm in town since mornin' and the wife will have my life.' But just in case he had any ideas concerning an extension of our good Samaritanship, we wished him a Happy Christmas and headed for our respective buses and home, that was really home: or in my case, what was about to become home.

It was a good Christmas too as I remember, but the little man remained in my mind, all through it. Was his wife really as stern as she seemed from his remark, and if she was what kind of unseasonable torture had she subjected him to throughout the day? Was he constantly reminded of his idiocy, or did she retreat into silence, sighing deeply as she ate her ham without benefit of turkey? I never saw him again, although I was often in the pubs around Henry Street. The thought crossed my mind, that the loss of the turkey, was the last straw, and from that Christmas Eve on, the poor little man in black was permanently barred from the city centre, and he had to sit in his suburban local, thinking of windows full of plump turkeys the whole length of Moore Street.

A Toast on the Eve

MICHEAL O'SIADHAIL

Where is the star that winks in the east?
In this the nadir of the year, we sense
the drag of time. For a while deceased
friends trouble us — a glum roundabout
of memory. O beg a freshborn innocence,
some star to blink beyond a doubt.

Where is the star that signals in the east?
Tonight I am both adult and child;
I shape and plan and still am an unleased
tenant of my clay, never master of my history.
Ambitious and humble, I am reconciled
to bear this double witness to a mystery.

Where is the star that beckons to the east,
that God come down to bless the flesh
of living? O give us the daily yeast
to burble through the veins and charm
our sour grapes into wine. Find me the crèche
where a God is cradled by woman's arm.

35

Where is the star that dances in the east?
Son of Ghost and Virgin forgive our meagre
welcome. Busy in the inns we feast
your arrival cribbed between ox and ass.
O give us our innocence, all green and eager.
To the God of renewal, I raise this glass.

Christmas Confession

EAMON KELLY

In Domhnall Bán Ó Céileachair's *Scéal mo Bheatha* he tells of hearing the old people in Coolea, talk about the drink they had after the supper on Christmas Eve. It seems the man of the house would put a small pot of spring water on the fire, not exactly full, but near enough to it. As it began to come to the boil, the whiskey jar was uncorked and poured into the bubbling pot, sugar and I forget what other condiments were added, and the whole concoction well stirred with a wooden spoon. When it was ready, members of the household, and if there were neighbours visiting, took whatever vessel was next to hand, a cup, a mug, a bowl, even a small saucepan, and dipping it into the pot and drinking, they toasted Christmas, and prayed all would be alive to enjoy another draft, the same time next year. They didn't go too far with the drink according to Domhnall Bán because of the religious nature of the occasion I suppose. But no doubt that punch was the perfect nightcap, and when the household hit the hay, they slept soundly, until they were called for first Mass on Christmas morning.

Religion played a far bigger part in Christmas that time than it does now. Even when I was a child, nearly every aspect of Christmas, Nollaig na bhFear, anyway, was centred around the nativity. For one thing there'd be a crib in every house. The four legged occupants of the crib, the cow the sheep and the ass, were no strangers to us. But we did wonder a bit all right, the first time we saw the camel making his appearance, on the feast of the three kings. Looking at the crib, the old people often recalled for us a time more than half a century before, when small-holders had to pay extra rent to the landlord if they built out-houses for their livestock, so that in the winter-time, animals, moreover those with young, like a sheep with Christmas lambs, a cow with her calf, maybe an ass or a mule, would be brought into the kitchen from the cold. Fear of the fox, was good enough reason for bringing in the ducks, and the few surviving geese, whose job it was to reproduce for next year. The hens were also tucked away in the coop from the maidrín rua, and we'll say now in the case of a recently married couple, with their first child in the cradle in the middle of all that menagerie on the straw covered floor, and we'll say too, if a stranger opened the door on Christmas night, well you couldn't blame him for thinking that he had been swept back in time, to the stable at Bethlehem, no angels of course, but I'd say they weren't far away!

But to bring you back to my own young days: confession was a great institution at that time, and wives and mothers coaxed, and if that didn't work, persuaded and even threatened their husbands and sons, to go and talk to the priest, when they were in the village or the nearest town on Christmas Eve. Very often the poor husband forgot his wife's warning, until he saw the cross on the gate of the Friar's Chapel on his way home. Up the steps he'd go and into the church, and after selecting the confession box where he'd get the best hearing, he'd 'skeet' his hat in along the seat, following the other penitents from pew to pew, examining his conscience for misdemeanours, as he went, until finally he'd come to the door of the confessional, where he'd go in, tell his sins, and make his peace with the man above.

The world and his wife would be at confession on Christmas Eve that time. All manner of people would be there, the old and the young, the sound and the sensible even those whom God, Glory be to Him, left without any 'splink', and one such man in my time was known as 'the carpenter'. He was a harmless likeable person who had served his time to carpentry before he went astray in himself. For months on end he'd be as level headed as Aristotle, until he was confronted with the pine smell of a new door, or a freshly made cart, then going into a bit of a dance, he'd take out his two foot rule and measure the door or the cart, calling out in a loud sing song, the height and the breadth of it, and the width and the thickness of the scantlings that went into its making. He was in the Friar's Chapel one Christmas Eve, the friars were replacing the old confession boxes at the time, and only one new box had been put in place so far, and this was the one 'the carpenter' made for. The friars weren't hearing, they'd just gone for a bit of a break, or maybe to sing a community hymn, and it was just as well, for when 'the carpenter' came face to face with the smell of the unvarnished wood of the newly made confessional, he went into a hop and a step, and slipping out his two foot rule, he began to measure the new door, and if there was anyone in the chapel that night in doubt as to the exact height and width of the door, that doubt was soon banished, when he heard 'the carpenter' calling: 'six foot and five-eights by two foot nine and three-quarters'.

The measuring of the door finished, 'the carpenter' disappeared into the priest's compartment. Luck of goodness the friar wasn't inside before him, and putting his head out through the purple curtain, he sang aloud the same as if he was giving out benediction the internal dimensions. Devout old ladies nearly lost their life when they saw and heard what was happening, but before he could climb to the top of the confessional, to measure the cross and just as the friars were coming back, two neighbours of his coaxed 'the carpenter' away to an old box, where calm and collected, he began to examine his conscience for confession.

First Mass in the morning saw him at the altar rails, and after in the half dark at the chapel gate, he joined his neighbours in the exchange of Christmas greetings. 'Happy Christmas men, happy Christmas everyone, and the blessings of God on us all!'

A Visit to the Manger

PAT INGOLDSBY

'Shhh! Up here . . . don't make a sound . . . up here
on the roof. Over this way. Easy does it . . . right . . .
you're up. Look . . . look down there. You can see
thro' this hole. Can you see it? It's a little baby in the
straw. I thought I was seeing things . . . the manger.
What? It's a boy. They're going to call him Jesus.
That's his mother there . . . look. Isn't she very young
and beautiful. She has a lovely face. That man beside
her . . . yeah . . . jigging up and down to stay warm
and blowing into his hands . . . he's the father . . .
Joseph. I've never seen anything like it. Look . . . the
cow . . . it's breathing on the infant to keep it warm.
Amazing. It must be freezing down there. That's no
place for a newly born baby. What? Why was he born
here? Well . . . they did the best they could . . . Mary
and Joseph . . . they did the best they could. Oooooh
look . . . just look at her face. Mary full of joy. She
looks so happy and proud. There are things she
doesn't know and it's just as well. Happy and proud
and that baby . . . Jesus . . . that baby in the straw is
going to change the whole world. No . . . I'm serious . . .

he is going to say things that are going to touch peoples' hearts in a way they have never been touched before. Ah no . . . not yet . . . give him a chance . . . sure he has to learn how to walk yet. Listen . . . he's crying . . . isn't that beautiful.

'His friends and family . . . they'll be the only ones at first. Nobody else will know anything about him. A carpenter's son . . . hammering and banging . . . belting his finger with the hammer . . . helping Joseph with the woodwork. Actually he'd be far better off if he stuck to the carpentry. A trouble-maker . . . that's what he'll be called. Rocking the boat . . . he's going to say an awful lot of things that people would rather not hear. If you've got two warm coats – give one of them away. I wouldn't mind one myself right now to be honest with you . . . it's freezing up here.

'Love . . . treating other people the way you'd wish to be treated yourself . . . feeding the hungry . . . housing the homeless . . . giving of yourself. Lots of people will call him crazy . . . how can you receive by giving? That's what he's going to say. You get by giving. No . . . it doesn't seem to make much sense . . . but he's going to keep right on saying it. Give away all your riches and follow me. People aren't going to like that one little bit.

'Hey! Look! Where did they come from? That's right . . . they look like shepherds . . . they should be out on the hills with the sheep. There's loads and loads of wolves out there. I wonder what they're doing. A lamb . . . look . . . one of them has got a lamb . . . and they're kneeling. Isn't that an extra-ordinary sight . . . grown men kneeling beside a new born baby. They know. It's no ordinary baby down there. They know. I wonder how much Mary knows?

'Hey! Will we give him a present? What have you got? The clothes you're standing up in! That's all I've got too.

'We could go down and wish Joseph and Mary all the best with the new baby. You'll sing him a song? Sure, why not. And I'll say a poem for him. My name is Pat from Malahide. What's yours? Simon . . . Simon from where? Cyrene . . . no I never heard of there . . . I'm delighted to meet you anyway. A song and a poem . . . grand . . . sure that's better than nothing. Hold on a second! We'll wait till the shepherds have gone. There's not much room down there.

'Would you look at that! They're laughing their heads off. I think Joseph said something. He's in great form and why not? And Mary . . . she looks on top of the world. Aren't you glad we're here . . . . Singing! Yeah . . . thanks be to goodness you can hear it too. I thought I was imagining things. No . . . I don't know where it's coming from. The sky is full of it. This is some night . . . you can say that again . . . this is some night.'

Sweet Dreams Rebecca

MICHEAL O'SIADHAIL

Sweet dreams, Rebecca!
Snug with milk, unfussed
by toys or tinsel, not yet
six weeks beyond the womb,
stranger, you still trust
the eastern star that beckons
towards the manger of sleep.

Goodnight, newcomer –
while all the merry gentlemen romp about the town
to pack the smoky inns,
down the season's compliments,
sing and warm their bones
around the bowl of fellowship.

All's well, my baby!
Adam model two
swaddled in his stable
sleeps deeply, so you

breathe easy as the donkey
whose breath puts out
an angel's flaming sword.

Goodnight, my girl!
Somewhere in the small hours
years ago another child
uncurls, hurries to discover
at the bed-end wise men's gifts,
frets and begs the light
unfurl a paradise of day.

Sleep long, my lovely!
It's December — Jerusalem
light years away. We bow
between our thanks and trust
and so re-enter, what you
Rebecca still remember:
Eden of the eternal now.

Malahide Memories on Christmas Eve

PAT INGOLDSBY

Somehow I always seem to find my way down here on Christmas Eve. Standing outside the door of the old house where I was born, and just a couple of steps away, the village green. It used to be the old village green in the heart of Malahide. I'm just looking out across the green at the grey sullen waters of the estuary, and over there my father used to row myself and my brothers and sisters across to the sand dunes on the island. Now they're silent and now they're still. And I find it very very easy to remember, standing down here underneath the very same bedroom window . . . my father used to creak that window open on Christmas Eve and look out and say — 'Listen boys . . . listen.'

We're sitting on the floor and there's a big fire in the hearth and my father isn't home yet and we're saying to my mother — 'When is Daddy coming home? When is Daddy coming home?' Christmas Eve seemed to go on forever and there was no sign of him and then he appeared very large in the doorway.

46

He had two little parcels under his arms and he gave them to us and we sat on the floor and unwrapped them. Inside each box was a perfect replica of a milk-float and my father had spent hours going around Dublin city looking for them while two little boys sat at home and wondered — 'This is Christmas Eve . . . where is he?' And that's where he was. That's my favourite memory of Christmas. Just thinking now about the time, the trouble and the love that one man put into finding two presents for two little boys.

Across the grey waters of the estuary there's only one or two boats tied up now and a very short distance across the water you can see the clouds bundled up against the sand dunes over on the island and way way off in the distance, just dimly discernible in the mist, the faint imperceptible outline of Lambay Island about nine miles off-shore. With all these childhood memories of Christmas flooding back around me here in the heart of old Malahide village I find it very easy to stand here now and cast my mind to Bethlehem.

47

Outsider

MICHEAL O'SIADHAIL

A sheltered arch or where underground
kitchens of an inn sent
through grids of pavement grating
the warmth of the ass's breath —
where did last night's Christ lie down?

Every morning for months I watched
a man I might have been,
about my age and bearded too,
his face blotched crimson
with cheap wine and sleeping rough.

He walked the far side of the street
always hurrying somewhere;
a father who couldn't praise, I wondered,
or what had blurred his star?
For months our eyes never met,

though the street between was narrow
until that eve he crossed.
'Some help,' he said, but it must have been
my double's eyes that asked
where would He lie down tomorrow?

An old outsider within winced,
shook him off and fled;
that street between was so narrow —
I chose the inn and was afraid.
I'm sure I've never seen him since

but tomorrow when carafes go round
a lone presence will pass
tremors through our frail togetherness;
again those eyes will ask
where did last night's Christ lie down?

A Mother's Christmas

HUGH LEONARD

My mother who never went abroad in her life was the owner of a passport. It was called Christmas, and it marked the completion of one journey and the beginning of another. To her Christmas was a way of saying — We've arrived, we're here, we've come through. Poverty, illness, worries, bills, all the dangers, the reefs, the storms, were passed. We were at anchor in a lagoon of quiet water before again venturing upon the high seas. And, like all passports, Christmas was not to be tampered with. Safety dwelt in its unwavering sameness. Every moment of the day itself was a re-run of the same moment a year ago, and would itself be repeated a year hence: the same paper chains, the same holly — well it looked the same — tucked behind what Dylan Thomas called the 'dickie-bird-watching pictures of the dead', the same bakelite crib on top of the television set, and there were the same neighbours, come for a bottle of stout or a glass of port so cloyingly sweet that at a sip one's lips all but fused together and the same visit after tea from my Uncle John and my Aunt Chris. We played 25s and ate cake. I hated the marzipan and hid it down my stocking leg, and my mother looking at her cards would inevitably moan: 'some one was hung in this chair', and just as surely my Aunt Chris would give her superior little laugh that was like a crystal wine glass and say, 'Oh Mag, what a remark to make!'

Now and again over the years, a neighbour would ask my mother if I took after her. She would look at me scowl and say darkly: 'Him? Sorry a bit of him, sure he's unnatural'. And yet I do take after her in one respect. For most of the year I plot and plan to be anywhere but at home, on a canal boat in France perhaps, or driving in Kerry across the high passes, or in New York or London or telling my wife that yes, she can have the nest of tables she once saw in Sorrento, if only she who hates travel will come with me to Capri. I have wanderlust, and yet Christmas must never change and it must happen at home. I enjoy even its unpleasant aspects — the crowds, the loudness of the pubs and when I go to the airport to meet my daughter home from London and the aircraft is an hour late I can even accept that as part of the immutable ritual, and on Christmas Day itself there is the morning walk along Vico Road and down Dalkey Avenue, the slivers of smoked salmon before lunch — now not lunch at all, but dinner, a great feast. And in the afternoon and evening, woe betide whomever is not a friend and yet comes to the door, for it is a day when the old epigram holds true; old books to read, old wine to drink, old wood to burn, old friends to keep. The family becomes a cocoon. If you were to venture outside, the streets are all but empty; a few children play with their new toys, and a car goes by bearing sons and sisters and cousins and in-laws from one family to the next; otherwise everyone is at home. It is as if the country had a million tiny hearts all warm and lightsome.

Christmas is of course a celebration of the Christian message, it is also that triumphant cry: 'We've arrived, we're here. We've come through.' It is one more visa stamped into the passport. I like to have my Christmases exactly the same, and I suspect that the reason is that the passport allows you to re-enter the most inaccessible of Kingdoms: the past. Change it and it becomes invalid; you're turned back at the frontier.

Christmas was Surely Coming

PAT INGOLDSBY

A horse and cart creaked and harness-clinked down the hill that was winter frost-breath morning. Another one followed behind. Christmas was surely coming and so too were the loads of logs and twigs from the castle. Logs and twigs that were cart-trundled on to the green in the middle of the village. A present from his lordship up in the castle. Me and my brother, we knew something about a lord who lived in a castle which was built by the Normans and it still had suits of armour in it. We liked that bit. We liked stepping out of our house with buckets as big as ourselves to collect up the logs and join all the people on the green and they'd be laughing because soon, the logs and twigs, they'd be crackling and spitting and burning and shadow-dancing on the ceiling. And Christmas was surely coming.

The green was right outside our house and on the other side of it, the frozen sea. The cold wind from it couldn't touch us now that the logs were in and my father and mother, they were shaking the dust off the paper chains, red and yellow and green and drawing-pinning them to the low wooden ceiling which they could touch easily without standing up on anything, but we couldn't. Large green paper balls that twisted and spun in every draught and your father lifted you up safe and sound to finger-tip them. And Christmas was surely coming.

Rabbits dangled down head-first outside the fish shop. Soon they'd be gone and then the turkeys. Holly rested on the saw-dusted floor and late at night me and my brother huddled close together in the bed because the wind off the sea made noises down the fire-less chimney in the corner of the room. And always in the late night we could smell fresh paint. Fresh paint? Who was painting when everyone was in bed? And my father, he'd finished clacking his typewriter downstairs hours ago. We never tiptoed down. We never set eyes on the fine young raven-haired man with the black moustache and his auburn slender wife painting with love — painting 'C.I.E.' and 'SUCK-A-ZUBE' on to the wooden double-decker bus. Carefully daubing 'JOHNSTON, MOONEY & O'BRIEN' on to the wooden bread van. We never heard the man hammering and banging and sawing weeks before, until the toys were well and truly ready because Christmas was surely coming. And upstairs we could smell the fresh paint.

We never saw the man as he really was. Young and black-haired. We never really saw the beautiful woman who would turn the heads when she took her wicker basket and did the shopping. We saw our father. We saw our mother. We see them now, as they were then, in the yellowing black and white and brown photographs. Is that the way they really were? We never knew. And soon the tree would be up, bent over at the top because the ceiling was so low, yet you could only touch it when he lifted you up.

Me and my brother together in the bed. 'Do you think he'll bring the . . . ? Do you think he knows where . . . ? Do you think there are ghosts in the chimney?' And when my father stood at the bedroom window and said: 'Boys, it won't be long now' – the ghosts in the chimney were gone. And so were we. To waken up to bare feet on cold linoleum floor and scamper downstairs and yes yes the tree is up and white-bowled, grease-proofed puddings cauldron-bubbled in the saucepans and our father said: 'I wouldn't be at all surprised if Santa brought you a C.I.E. bus and a Johnston Mooney & O'Brien bread-van.'

'Because . . . because we asked him for it?'

'Because you asked him for it.'

Santa must have got the letter!

My father stood beside the bedroom window on the night you were so excited that you couldn't sleep and the white pillow-cases were at the end of the bed and the ghosts were gone from the chimney and he eased down the window on the sash and we could hear the sea on the other side of green. Then my father said it: 'Boys . . . listen . . . over on the island. Santa's sleigh bells.' And we listened and we heard them just as surely as if they were there. We heard them . . . he was on the way . . . and we'd better . . . we'd better go asleep.

He got the note! He got the letter! Suck-A-Zube and the bread-van! The logs hissed and crackled safe warmth and always after dinner on Christmas Day my father said it — 'go mbeidhmís beo ar an am seo arís.'

And we were. But then, he wasn't. And we love him. Because Christmas is coming. And as long as it surely is . . . we surely will.

Originally published in The Evening Press.

The Season of Light

EAMON KELLY

No word of a lie but Christmas was something to
write home about when I was small. Oh! the way we
looked forward to twilight on Christmas Eve, for
when darkness fell it was Christmas Night, the greatest
night of all the year. We youngsters would be up with
the crack of dawn that morning to have the house
ready for the night.

Berry holly would have to be cut and brought in to
deck out the windows, the top of the dresser, the
back of the settle and the clevvy. We'd bring in ivy
too and put a sprig of laurel behind the pictures,
above the lintel of the door and around the fireplace.
But we wouldn't overdo it, for if we did my mother
would make us cut it down a bit, reminding us that
she'd like to feel that she was in her own house for
Christmas, and not in the middle of a wood!

Well, the transformation we could bring about in
the kitchen with all that greenery! But we weren't
finished yet. The Christmas candles had to be pre-
pared; these were of white tallow as thick as the
handle of a spade and nearly as tall. In some houses

they'd scoop out a hole in a turnip and put the candle sitting into it. A big crock we'd use. We'd put the candle standing into that and pack it around with sand. If you hadn't sand, bran or pollard would do.

When the candle was firm in position we'd spike sprigs of holly or laurel into the sand about the candle, and we had coloured paper too to put around the outside of the crock to take the bare look off it. With that same coloured paper, the girls in the family, if they were anyway handy, could make paper flowers to decorate the holly. Then what could cap it all, was a length of young ivy and spiral it up around the candle — it looked lovely! That done, we would go through the same manoeuvre until there was a candle in a crock for every window in the house.

Then we'd be praying for night to fall, for you couldn't see the right effect until the candles were lit. That honour would fall to the youngest in the house. My father would lift him up saying: 'In the name of the Father and of the Son . . .' and when the child had blessed himself, he would put the lighting spill to the candle, and from that candle the other candles would be lit, and we'd be half daft with excitement, enjoying the great blaze of light, and running from the rooms to the kitchen and out into the yard to see what the effect was like from the outside. When we'd get tired of looking at the candles in our own windows, we'd turn and try to name the neighbours' houses as the bunches of lights came on, two windows here and three windows there, across the dark countryside and

away up to the foot of the hills. And as sure as anything someone'd be late and we'd rush into my
mother saying: 'Faith, then there's no light on yet in
Rossacrew!'

'Go on ye're knees!' my mother would say. The
time she'd pick for the rosary, just as the salt ling was
ready and the white onion sauce and the potatoes
steaming over the fire. But I suppose there'd be no
religion in the world only for the women. The rosary
in our house didn't end at five decades. Not at all.
After the Hail Holy Queen my mother would branch
into the trimmings:

'Come Holy Ghost send down those beams,
Which sweetly flow in silent streams'.

She'd pray for everyone in sickness and in need:
the poor souls and the sinful soul that was at that very
moment trembling before the judgement seat above.
She'd pray for the sailor on the seas: 'Protect him
from the tempest, Oh Lord, and bring him safely
home'. And the lone traveller on the highway and of
course our emigrants and, last of all, the members of
her own family:

'God bless and save us all.
St Patrick, Bridget and Colmcille
Guard each wall.
May the Queen of heaven
And the angels bright
Keep us and our house
From all harm this night!'

Our knees'd be aching as we got up off the floor, and it would take my father a while to get the prayer arch out of his back. Well, we wouldn't be sitting down to the supper when my mother'd bless herself again, a preliminary to grace before meals, and you could hardly blame my father for losing his patience.

'Is it in a monastery we are?' he'd say. 'Haven't we done enough praying for one night?'

After the supper there was Christmas cake for anyone with a sweet tooth. My father'd never look at that. His eye'd be on the big earthenware jar below the dresser, and it would be a great relief to him when my mother'd say to us: 'Go out there, one of ye, and tell the neighbouring men to come in for a while.'

It was the custom that night, Nollaig Mhór, big Christmas, for the men to visit each other's houses. The women were too busy to be bothered. They had their own night, 'Nollaig na mBan,' small Christmas, for making tapes. In a while's time the men'd come, and at the first lag in the conversation my father'd take the cork off the jar and fill out a few cups of porter. The men, by the way, not noticing what was going on, and then when they'd get the cups, all surprise they'd say: 'What's this? What's this for?'

'Go on take it,' my father'd say. 'It is Christmas night, neighbours, and more luck to us!'

Then the men's faces'd light up and lifting their cups they'd say: 'Happy Christmas, Ned: Happy Christmas, ma'am! Happy Christmas, everyone!'

'And the same to ye men,' my father would answer. 'May we all be alive again this time twelve months.'

And my mother, who was never very happy in the presence of strong drink, would direct her gaze in the direction of the Christmas candle and say:

'The grace of God to us all!'

Originally published in The Rub of a Relic *by Eamon Kelly, The Mercier Press, 1978.*

The Aunts

VAL MULKERNS

The aunts tended to become a little quarrelsome after their port and plum pudding and my mother didn't like it. She would say reprovingly 'Christmas Day' in that tone that years later I knew Stephen Dedalus' mother had used when her visitors fatally brought up the subject of Parnell. The aunts who had come to us for Christmas dinner weren't quarrelling about Parnell, although, mind you, I did hear one of them mention him with approval which the other didn't share.

No, our maiden aunts, we'll call them Molly and Ivy, started to squabble about more immediate things. This was some time around the early 1930s and my grandmother had recently died so after her second glass of this special port my father was given every Christmas by one of his customers Molly would begin fretfully, 'At all events poor mother's writing desk should, by rights, have come to me, everyone expected it would and besides . . .'

'Besides dear,' Ivy would chip in, 'you got the best of the Foxford blankets and *A Sacrifice of Vanities* and then nothing would do you but to pick out . . . '

'That's quite enough,' my mother would say firmly, 'on Christmas Day. Jimmy can't you think of something?' This last in an aside to my father.

Molly would press on regardless. 'Those silver apostle spoons were mine I'd have you know because I happen to have bought them at Dan Ryan's auction and besides . . .'

'Even Mad Carew,' my mother would mutter urgently although this recitation was not one of her favourites.

My father would smile expansively in the candle-light which threw shadows of his special autumn leaf decorations on the ceiling. We never had a Christmas tree. They were expensive, and few and far between when I was a child but we had fairy lights in the hall because my father worked for the General Electric Company and somewhere he had bought this big box of imitation autumn leaves made from canvas, I think, and painted in the hectic colours of Virginia creeper.

'Very well then,' my father would say after pouring the women more port and helping himself to a 'tincture' (as he called it) of John Jameson. At this stage he was always mellow and pleased with himself. He had done the right thing and had had the aunts once again for Christmas Day when everybody else had backed down. Now he was going to entertain them further, for good measure. They had heard the king's speech as they requested and after that they had grown a little tired of the wireless. 'Too noisy' they said, in agreement for once.

Now it so happens that at this stage of my emotional

development I hadn't heard of the Troubadours and I thought 'The Green Eye of the Little Yellow God,' the height of romantic love. I was seven or eight years of age, given to poring over old theatre programmes and play scripts, for want of something better to read and I knew that before my father had begun to sell electric goods to support his family he had been something in the theatre as well as something in the Southern and Great Western Railway. In fact I learned only a short time ago from Sean O'Mahony's book on Frongoch that even before 1916 my father ran a troop of travelling entertainers called 'Palmer and Rimlock'. I also know, because he mentioned it so often, that for a small part in the Abbey he had actually taken elocution lessons from Frank Fay, or was it Willie, and I had reason to know that he aimed to get value for his money by teaching me.

'Shoulders back, head up and speak from the diaphragm', he would say and set me reading from *The Land of Hearts Desire* or something like that. If I wasn't very lucky I'd be called on myself to entertain the aunts so I clapped him loudly and moreover thumped my two young brothers into clapping him too. He didn't need much encouragement but he did like to finish his cigar first. Some customer or other always gave him cigars for Christmas, the only time he could afford to smoke them, so there are those leafy shadows on the ceiling and bright firelight and a thick white candle sinking lower into the holly and red ribbons and there's this smell of cigars and John

Jameson and there's my father throwing back his foxy head of hair to begin the tale of the dashing red-headed hero who dared all for love of the colonel's daughter and lost.

There's a one eyed yellow idol in the town
    of Katmandu,
There's a little marble cross below the town,
There a broken hearted woman tends the
    grave of Mad Carew,
And the yellow god forever watches down.

Those lines always made me want to cry a bit but I'd have died myself rather than admit it. I would be lying face downwards on the hearth rug so that no-body would notice the red eyes when I lifted a face that was red too above a red tartan Christmas dress. But my father knew and he winked at me above the applause and the aunts so far forgot their quarrel that they called for 'Sam Magee' to follow and the anti-recruiting song he had written in 1913 to follow that. It was called 'Come along and join the British Army' and just to remind them he could sing another sort of song I knew 'The Pride of Petravore', that story of foolish Eileen Óg would follow and I didn't mind because I knew that at seven or eight years of age I was well, a little bit in love with my father, especially on Christmas Day.

Originally broadcast on RTE's Sunday Miscellany, *produced by Maxwell Sweeney.*

This December Day

BRENDAN KENNELLY

Here in this room, this December day,
Listening to the year die on the warfields
And in the voices of children
Who laugh in the indecisive light
At the throes that but rehearse their own
I take the mystery of giving in my hands
And pass it on to you.

I give thanks
To the giver of images,
The reticent god who goes about his work
Determined to hold on to nothing.
Embarrassed at the prospect of possession
He distributes leaves to the wind
And lets them pitch and leap like boys
Capering out of their skin.
Pictures are thrown behind hedges,
Poems skitter backwards over cliffs,
There is a loaf of bread on Derek's threshold
And we will never know who put it there.

For such things
And bearing in mind
The midnight hurt, the shot bride,
The famine in the heart,
The demented soldier, the terrified cities
Rising out of their own rubble,

I give thanks.

I listen to the sound of doors
Opening and closing in the street.
They are like the heartbeats of this creator
Who gives everything away.
I do not understand
Such constant evacuation of the heart,
Such striving towards emptiness.

Thinking, however, of the intrepid skeleton,
The feared definition,
I grasp a little of the giving
And hold it close as my own flesh.

It is this little
That I give to you.
And now I want to walk out and witness
The shadow of some ungraspable sweetness
Passing over the measureless squalor of man
Like a child's hand over my own face
Or the exodus of swallows across the land

And I know it does not matter
That I do not understand.

Originally published in Salvation, the stranger, *Tara Telephone Publications: Gallery Books, Dublin 1972.*

Tonight There are No Trains

PAT INGOLDSBY

He walked a lot. Christmas Day walking . . . any-where . . . not wanting to walk back to his room. No . . . not yet . . . not until late . . . time enough later. Once he had walked Christmas Day in the woodlands, twigs crackling, scarves and gloves, brothers and sisters laughing, white clouds, frozen breath, mother at home. Silent Night. God, it's silent now anyway.

The bedsit house is quiet, empty. All gone home for Christmas. Nobody back yet, doors locked, gone away. Red green paper-chain hanging down in the hall. Torn and moving in the draught. Follow a star, rent a room, go home for Christmas.

His alarm clock ticking him towards bedtime. A car passing outside in the dark. Not stopping. Heading far away from this empty silent-night house where his window is the only one with curtains drawn, keeping the light in . . . shutting the wind and the dark out. Car – where are you going?

In the morning he walked down to Mass . . . frost, children.

'Hey look! Look what he brought me . . . no – honestly,

68

I wasn't awake, Gerry was, he saw him, a beard, a white beard, honest!'

This must be the Mystical Body, everybody heading in the same direction. The church, this must be it. If only all of us who are walking down in ones, singly . . . if only . . . a group, all of us together instead of . . .

Looking in through other people's windows . . . look, Christmas trees, a father playing piggy-back with little giggling ringlets, holding a teddy bear. That fire looks warm. Oh God – see how its red and blue and green dances on the coloured balls. Can I come in? You know . . . be a part of your family, your Christmas tree, children playing, I won't get in the way. Log crackling . . . deck . . . deck the what? Oh yeah – the boughs.

He walked on.

The church. Kneeling in the back row. See the backs of heads, here, there and everywhere. Floor vibrates, organ booms and choir, crystal-clear voices. 'Round yon Virgin Mother and Child, Holy Infant so tender and . . .'

Little heads, lots and lots of little heads swinging around, the choir's up there somewhere, maybe in heaven.

'What did I tell you, don't look around, you're in the church, Holy God's house, you can't look around in here, Holy God will be very very cross. It's Christmas Day, say your prayers.'

Those children, are they looking at me? He did want to pray. It's just he couldn't find the words, the right ones. The only words he found – 'God – where's my woodland brothers and sisters walking now? And on the white ceiling we did, we pinned up the green paper balls. You better be in bed early and asleep, go asleep or he won't come, he won't. That's right, the glass of milk and the minced pie, put it there, he'll need that, he'll be very hungry. God – where is it now? Who drank the milk? Did you?'

He did want to pray but you can't pray like that.

You . . . you over there, can I come and kneel with you, the two of you, you'd be on both sides of me and I'd be in the middle. Good King what? Will you move over? I won't be any trouble. When the Mass is finished I will, I'll go my own way and I'll deck the boughs, honestly I will, I'll deck them . . . someplace else.

The priest gave a sermon. 'My dear children.' All about families, The Holy One, your one. Oh yeah, my one. Husbands, love your wives. Wives, would you like to come back to my place for a coffee? No, there's no cake. There's no people, they're all gone, but we can talk, it's warm, I got a new gas cylinder to take me over the holidays. The shops are shut.

'Take this and eat it,' said the priest.

It's been a long time. Do you remember when we did? The priest said we'd all pray for a change of heart, God never stops loving you even when you've pulled the curtains to keep the light in and the dark out and the paper chain is swinging in the hall.

The signal box beside the level-crossing is in darkness. He felt sorry that the man wasn't in there, smoking his pipe, turning the big wheel that swings the gates across, a train rushing past, clickedly clacking blur of brightly-lit people staring, windows, but tonight there are no trains . . . to anywhere.

'Do you, do you read books?' The old man asked him that, beside the level-crossing, whiskey breath, Christmas Day, whiskey breath.

'Take this and drink from it.' Whiskey bottle. 'Would you have a couple of shillings? You can have me book if you want it, there's no pictures in it or anything and I can't read, I found it.'

He took the book, a present, a Christmas present from Whiskey-breath. I'll bring it back to my room and I'll read it.

'What? A few bob? . . . oh yeah . . . a few bob . . .'

Goodnight to you children playing piggy-back in the front room. Goodnight to you Christmas trees and crackling logs. Goodnight cars, going somewhere, not stopping. Paper chain, I'll find a drawing pin and I'll fix you up again and sure that'll look much better and then, then perhaps I'll sleep. The woodlands might be there and I'll crack twigs 'till the morning comes.

Out on the Road

EAMON KELLY

Only once ever did it happen that I was out of Ireland for Christmas. That time I was in America and after playing on Broadway we went out on the road on tour spending a week at a time in each big city. The week before Christmas found us in Wilmington, Delaware. Christmas Eve fell on a Saturday that year and we, the Irish section of the theatre company, were dumbfounded to hear that we would be working on Christmas Eve. And not alone that but we would have to do two shows — one at 5 and one at 8 — what is known in the trade as a back-to-back. We consoled ourselves that America wasn't Ireland, where Christmas Eve and Holy Week meant closed doors as far as the theatre was concerned.

On arrival in Wilmington some of us opted to stay in a motel on the outskirts of the city and you couldn't ask for nicer weather as we drove into the theatre in the Dupont Complex for the first show on Christmas Eve. We played to a full house, and a meal and a rest were the order of the day when the show was over, so that we didn't have time to venture out into the city to see what the weather was like before the curtain went up again at 8 o'clock. Like the first house the second was also full and I couldn't help wondering, remembering what Christmas Eve was like in my young days in Ireland, if the people had any homes to go to or any decorations to put up for the festive season but knowing Americans I'd say all that had been done already.

As the play progressed I found it hard to keep my thoughts from wandering back across the sea to Christmases long ago at home. The play we were in was Brian Friel's celebrated *Philadelphia, Here I Come* and there is a scene at the opening of the third act where the family kneel down to say the rosary on young Gar's last night at home before going to America. As the Our Fathers and the Hail Marys, and the responses to same, swelled and died in a sleep inducing drone, the young emigrant's thoughts soared west over the Atlantic as he visualises what life is going to be like for him in Philadelphia far away. But on this Christmas Eve in Wilmington as young Gar's thoughts soared west from Ireland my thoughts were soaring too, but in the opposite direction to our own house in Carrigeen, Glenflesk.

How clear it all became to me, every detail of the kitchen, the picture of the holy family, the berry holly, the laurel and the ivy decorating the walls, the mottoes on the chimney breast, the roaring fire, the Christmas candles in the windows, bringing what was to us at that time a glorious blaze of light. Images of Christmas at home crowded the mind when we as children sat around the fire eating Christmas cake and hanging a stocking on the crane for Daidí na Nollag to put maybe a mouth organ, a jew's harp, a whistle, a new penny or a rosy apple into it. We'd know in the morning and if Santa supplied the instruments you'd hear music of a sort as we drove to early Mass in the pony and trap. The sound of hooves on the frosty roads, the loud salutations at the chapel gate as neighbours exchanged Christmas greetings echoed and re-echoed in my head. 'Your decade', from Madge, the housekeeper in the play, brought young Gar back from his dreams and me back to reality. The reality that was S. B. O'Donnell's stage kitchen in Wilmington, Delaware.

When we came out of the theatre that night the city was blanketed in snow and strangely quiet as whatever little traffic there was seemed to glide soundlessly over the white streets. We had some trouble in getting a taxi. Those at the centre of the city didn't want to venture to the outskirts in case they couldn't get back, for now the snow was coming down again and slanting in the rising wind. Eventually we were lucky enough to get an empty cab going in our direction. When we got out the snow had piled so high against the walls of the motel I had to brush it away to find the door handle, and when the door opened inwards there was a wall of snow almost three feet high between me and the room. By scooping it outwards with my bare hands, a bit like a rabbit setting about making a burrow, I managed to get in without bringing too much snow with me.

Oh! I'll never forget the feeling of loneliness that came over me as I shut the door and looked around the bare motel room. Granted the bed was comfortable, and there was a dressing-table, a wardrobe, a john and shower but one picture would have brightened the place up. Just one picture with a sprig of berry holly behind it! Grin and bear it was the only thing. The night would soon pass and tomorrow, Christmas Day, at the crack of dawn we would be on the road again to Chicago, Illinois, 1,000 miles away, where we'd open on Stephen's Day. No rest for the wicked.

I got into bed thinking of the early morning run to the airport in the wake of the snow-ploughs I had heard about. Then in the plane, in the wake of the flame-throwing gadgets which cleared the snow and ice from the runways and then in the air, watching below me as the land changed from white to the brown winter terrain of the Mid West where, according to the weather reports, there was no snow yet but there might be before morning.

Just then the phone rang. A fellow player who couldn't sleep no more than myself had rounded up some American and Irish actors from the cast and would I come down to the lobby? Would a dog bark? Parcels of good cheer meant for dear friends in Chicago were rifled, I'm afraid. Those of us with wives and families rang them up, greetings on the line, as Christmas Eve merged into Christmas Day, toasts were drunk, songs were sung and stories were told of Christmases long ago when the world was young and we were happy sitting by our own firesides.

The Wren-Boy

BRENDAN KENNELLY

The little eagle-conquering wren has died
For him, tautly poised on the threshold there.
Gaunt in his fomorian pride
White feathers in his hair
Swaddled in gold and green
His right fist flicks the swarthy stick
And beats the goatskin tambourine.

The majesty of Stephen's Day
Is on his face, grown proud as Lucifer
As he begins to play.
Lithe bodies stir
To his music, cries
Of praise unfold and
Fierce pride leaps in his eyes.

As the ancient drumbeat rings
From beaten skin, he steps
Into the days of unremembered kings;
Alone, he tops

This day of hectic moments in a flood
Of notes, their gay swashbuckling passion
Crashing through his blood.

Christmas townlands wait,
Carrig, Lenamore,
Road and field, they undulate
To every open door;
Village, byre and frosty ways
Show farmer, townie, whining crone
Grow generous with praise.

He knows dominion now
And leaves behind
The heavy spade, the ponderous plough
For glory in the mind
And blood; a man whose pride
In stick and drum commemorates
The bird that died.

Originally published in My Dark Fathers, *New Square Publications, Dublin 1964.*

A Convent at Christmas Time

BRYAN MacMAHON

My story comes from a convent at Christmas time and it concerns a pair of novices or, as they were known to the other nuns, two 'White Veils'. It happened in the mid 1920s.

The novices–girls of 17 or 18 or so, came from a seaside village in Kerry and were childhood friends. For a long time previous to this they had been discussing entering a convent together: at last when the local races were over, amid tears and laughter, they set off to devote their life to the service of others.

The convent they were about to enter was in a quiet small town, a big village it could be called, in the Irish Midlands: in character it was in total contrast to the village the girls had left behind with all its traditions manifest especially at Christmas time.

The novices were graciously received by the community. As October slid into November and November into December with Christmas coming up the girls were reasonably happy: they had the excitement of the nativity play in the school, the concert with the children, and the coming and going of visitors to occupy their minds. Suddenly it was Christmas Eve.

During this time their thoughts had turned to Bethlehem: indeed they experienced little home-sickness as they were kept busy. So what with the cards from home, the midnight Mass, the crib, the White Veils had plenty to think about. They *did* miss the candlelight in the windows of the hill cottages on Christmas Eve but set the loss aside.

On Christmas Day there was the usual dinner followed by a gentle relaxation of the rules. Towards evening the two White Veils looked into each other's eyes. 'Tomorrow,' they said, 'the boys and girls of our parish will go out in the Wren.' They said this almost without speaking.

The following day was St Stephen's Day. One of the novices put the homesickness into words. 'They'll be dressing up now at Murphy's,' she said, 'the girls in the room and the boys in the kitchen. There will be a snatch of music, the beat of the bodhrán: then with painted faces, out they will all go into the great adventure of the frosted countryside.'

A common thought occurred to the two White Veils. The basket of costumes from the nativity play was still in the schoolroom. 'Dare we?' was answered by — 'We dare.' They stole out of the silent convent, went around to the back of the school and entered the classroom where the basket was. The lid of the basket creaked open. The girls looked at the coloured finery of the east. They donned yashmaks and saris, they

80

changed their devotional veils for mysterious gauze, they painted their faces. One found a concertina — then again: 'Dare we?' was answered by 'We dare.'

Out into the village street they went. They danced and sang. The villagers were taken aback: there was no tradition whatsoever of the Wren in that place.

After an hour or so the pair again looked into each other's eyes. 'Dare we?' was again answered by 'We dare.'

Up past the white statue to the main door of the convent they went. They rang the bell. The concertina gave forth a wheezey jig as the door was opened by the Mother of Novices.

The bishop looked down from his purple picture. The statue in the hallway seemed aghast as the pair played and danced on the polished floor. The performance was at its height when the Mother of Novices shot forth her hand and gripped the musician's wrist. The tell-tale silver ring of the novitiate had given the game away.

Carpeted before the sleepy Reverend Mother in the parlour the pair looked at each other. 'Are we to be packed home?' was the question uppermost in their minds.

'I'll deal with this,' the Reverend Mother said severely as the door closed behind the Mother of Novices. The old nun's eyes that had been stern, slowly misted over. She looked out of the window for a long while. Then, 'I too went out in the Wren,' she said. 'I too missed it on my first Christmas here. But it is one of the joys we have to leave behind.'

Eyes downcast, the girls murmured, 'Yes Mother.'
'Off with you now,' the Old Reverend Mother said,
'and don't you dare do it again.'

The Best Christmas Present

CLARE BOYLAN

The best Christmas present I ever got was a giant-sized chocolate rabbit. I was about four at the time. The rabbit was the finest piece of sculpture I had ever seen and possibly the largest structure in chocolate in the world. It had a radiant grin, and arms outstretched in a gesture of worship or embrace. I thought it was wonderful. I would no more have eaten it than I would have roasted my grandmother.

The problem was my sisters. They thought all food was for eating. They even tried to eat my birthday cake which I kept in a tin under my bed all year and watched while it adjusted to the seasons with a decent overcoat of green fur. My sisters would eat tripe, or pigs' feet or tapioca, they would savage the marzipan santa off the Christmas cake or swallow without a squeak the red thing from a jar of pickles. I had a number of hiding places. Flat food such as bars or banana sandwiches I kept under my pillow, small lumpy items like dolly mixtures were secreted in a specially engineered hole under the wing of a cloth duck. Chocolates I tucked into the toe of a pair of pink wellingtons to eat while the family said the rosary. Trying to hide a giant-sized chocolate rabbit was like attempting to conceal a wanted criminal. There was nowhere in the house where he could be safely stowed without danger of being melted, sat upon, or found. In the end I settled for somewhere he could be seen but not touched. I put him in the Christmas crib.

The crib had been made by my father and was displayed during Advent on the hall table, lit up with Christmas lights. It was an all family endeavour. Each year we were invited to contribute something of our own devising and my sisters had already made shooting stars out of silver foil and paper angels dangling from threads. They were years older than me and were forever whittling and moulding and ironing the lids of milk bottles. For once I had something significant to offer.

'Ma,' my sisters yelled in unison. 'What is it?' my mother said quite crossly to the trouble-making older girls and then, in genuine awe, as she observed the burly chocolate figure, one ear jammed against the thatch, poised on a single paw, rapturous but perilous above the infant Jesus.

'It's St Joseph,' I said.

I did have a genuine confusion about the crib. It seemed to me to have an all animal cast. For years I had been lifted up and introduced to the cow and the ox and some sheep with lovely names like Frankincense and Myrrh. All the stories that were read aloud to me featured animal heroes. My mother now tried to set me straight on the Christmas story but I refused to be convinced — as far a I was concerned the old man and the lady in blue were looking after the Holy Family and the sleeping child was somebody's little brother.

The rabbit remained. The crib was removed from the hall table and placed in the bottom of the wardrobe. At last it seemed St Joseph was safe. Several days later we had a visit from Miss Thing who did our laundry. She was under-privileged and we were always told to be nice to her. In an excess of festive kindness I decided to show her St Joseph. Unlike my family she seemed genuinely impressed.

'Lovely,' she said, and her jaws opened wide in wonder and she bit off the rabbit's hind quarters. I was speechless. I stood there nursing the bottomless chocolate giant until Miss Thing had departed and then I howled like a banshee.

Feather Beds

JOHN B. KEANE

And now for a look at feather beds and how helpful they were in the matter of inducing sleep, sweet dreams and what have you. Feather beds were also the scourge of insomnia. It was the down of the goose that was used to stuff the tick and the younger the goose the better. Green geese they were called although some people used call them Michaelmas geese and would eat them on Michaelmas Day.

The plucks of all the geese killed over the years would be made into a tick for Christmas and presented to newly-weds on Christmas Eve. Let us however proceed with our examination of the feather bed proper. They used to say in Renagown in the Stacks Mountains that children born in feather beds had more nature in them than children born in mattresses. If this is true then I am most fortunate for I was born in a feather bed or so my mother told me.

The feather beds I recall from my youthful Christmases in the Stacks Mountains seemed never to be cold when one went between the sheets on frosty nights. One sunk at once into the downy depths of the tick and sleep came instantly.

Honeymoon couples who departed from the Stacks Mountains after the wedding breakfast would always spend one night in a contiguous town which boasted a hotel. One-day honeymoons were the vogue in country places up to and including the Second World War. Then young people became better off and more venturesome and would spend as long as a week on a honeymoon; a time would come when they would spend two.

In those far off days the one-day honeymooners would choose their hotel carefully. Money was scarce and they sought the best value available. The question uppermost in their minds would be whether or not the hotel was possessed of feather beds; if not the newly married pair would go further and would settle for no less than a tick stuffed with the best goose down. There were many reasons for this. In the first place they had been used to ticks all their lives. In the second place mattresses and spring beds made a great deal of noise whereas the feather bed made no sound whatsoever. This is why they appealed most to honeymooners.

I once overheard a conversation between two Listowel women; one accused the other of being a millionairess no less. It transpired that the accused party had a bed and breakfast establishment where she did a thriving business across the year.

'That's all right,' she said. 'But beds makes no battle with honeymooners.' Now what was implied here was that beds would have to be replaced fairly quickly due to the night-time and even day-time activities of honeymoon couples. Since new beds cost money it could be argued that the purchase of new ones would greatly diminish the profits from bed and breakfast. I was tempted to butt into the conversation and make the following suggestion; why not invest in a few feather ticks, those incomparable shock absorbers and silencers of bed noises whatever they might be. I kept my mind to myself however because I did not want to be accused of eavesdropping.

Also in my childhood there was much demand for pillows which had been stuffed with goose down. They used to say that if you rested your head on a feather pillow you would always dream of the girl you loved. The feather bed itself however had no peer and I lately placed an order with a country relative for a feather tick which should be ready for Christmas.

Now there are two interesting stanzas from two different ballads pertaining to beds. One goes like this:

> We courted under a rick
> In the mild and the wild of weathers
> And we loved on a downy tick
> Of green goose feathers

It is quite clear that the author was unequivocally in favour of the feather bed, that he spent his honeymoon in such a bed and that he was glad to be in it.

A second stanza is also composed by a honey-mooner as will be seen. It was written over seventy years ago by the late Bill Taylor of Athea in West Limerick. We shall see how the male of the honey-moon pair, without realising it, underscored the advantages of the feather bed although there is no mention of feathers in the stanza. He writes as follows:

We arrived in Athea at a quarter to one,
And up to the clergy we quickly did run,
It was there we were married, and without
    much delay
We burst a spring bed that night in Athea.

Now if he had insisted upon a feather bed his case would not have been called throughout the countryside but we would have been deprived of a very fine ballad indeed. Still it must by now be patently clear to all that the feather bed was without peer in the business of honeymooning which calls for the utmost discretion from the beginning to the end of the undertaking.

There is of course another beautiful ballad, the 'Ballad of Patsy McCann,' which if memory serves me correctly was written by Johnny Patterson:

Patsy McCann will you marry me daughter?
Patsy McCann will you take her to wed?
Ten golden sovereigns down I will give you,
A three-legged stool and a fine feather bed.

There is of course a good deal more but this is sufficient for this particular purpose which is to show the *meas* set by our ancestors in feather beds. It surely is time for us to put our goose plucks together and assemble the making of a fine feather bed for Christmas.

The Contributors

COLIN MORRISON is a senior producer with RTÉ. His productions have included *The Gay Byrne Show*, *The Pat Kenny Show*, *Airs and Races* and *Late Date*, as well as numerous documentaries and programmes with the RTÉ concert orchestra. His international awards include the Ondas Radio Award in Spain and the Premier Producer Prize in the Nordring Radio Competition for his production to mark the Joyce Centenary in 1982.

JOHN B. KEANE is one of Ireland's most popular authors and is recognised as a major Irish playwright. He has written many bestsellers including *Letters of an Irish Parish Priest*, *Letters of a Love-Hungry Farmer*, *Letters of a Matchmaker*, *Irish Short Stories*, *Man of the Triple Name*, *The Bodhrán-Maker*. His plays include *The Field*, *Big Maggie*, *Sive* and *Many Young Men of Twenty*.

MICHEAL O'SIADHAIL is a widely read and respected poet. His collections include *Springnight* and *The Image Wheel*. He was awarded the Irish American Cultural Institute's prize for poetry. He has been a lecturer at Trinity College, Dublin and a professor at the Dublin Institute for Advanced Studies. He is the editor of *Poetry Ireland Review* and a member of the Arts Council.

EAMON KELLY is Ireland's greatest and best-loved Seanchaí. He has worked with the Radio Éireann Players, the Gate Theatre and since 1967 he has been with the Abbey Theatre. He has been on Broadway and brought his storytelling show *In My Father's Time* to America. He has appeared on television in Ireland and England. His published works include *In My Father's Time, Bless Me Father, The Rub of a Relic* and *According to Custom.*

PAT INGOLDSBY'S plays have been broadcast on RTÉ and have been performed at The Peacock Theatre, The Gaiety Theatre, The Project Art Centre and The National Theatre. He has published five collections of poetry and is very successful writer of children's books. He presents his own show for children on television and he writes a weekly humorous column for *The Evening Press.*

SEAMUS HEANEY is one of Ireland's best known poets. He has won numerous awards for his poetry and has recently been appointed as Professor of Poetry at Oxford University. His published works include *Death of a Naturalist, Door into the Dark, Station Island, Wintering Out, The Haw Lantern,* and two collections of critical prose, *Preoccupations* and *The Government of the Tongue.*

HUGH LEONARD is one of Ireland's major dramatists. He has written also for British and American theatres and television. His plays include *Da, A Leap in the Dark, Stephen D, The Poker Session, Time Was, Kill, Some of My Best Friends are Husbands.* His film scripts include *Great Catherine, Herself Surprised* and *Troubles* and his books include *Leonard's Last Book, Home Before Night* and *Out After Dark.*

BREANDÁN Ó hEITHIR is a well-known broadcaster and columnist. His published works include *Willie the Plain Pint agus an Papa, Lig Sinn i gCathú (Lead Us into Temptation), The Begrudger's Guide to Irish Politics, Over the Bar* and *Sionnach ar mo Dhuán.*

VAL MULKERNS is a novelist, short shory writer, broadcaster and occasional lecturer. Her novel *The Summerhouse* won the AIB Prize for Literature in 1984. Other recent books include *Very Like a Whale* (1986) and *A Friend of Don Juan* (1988). She has been widely anthologised, most recently in *The Oxford Book of Irish Short Stories* edited by William Trevor.

BRENDAN KENNELLY is Professor of Modern Literature in Trinity College, Dublin. A leading Irish poet, his published works include *My Dark Fathers, Dream of a Black Fox, Love Cry, The Voices, A Small Light, Selected Poems, Cromwell, Moloney Up and At It* and *Love of Ireland — Poems from the Irish.* He introduced and edited *The Penguin Book of Irish Verse.*

BRYAN MacMAHON is best know for his short stories and his published collections include *The Lion Tamer, The Red Petticoat* and *The Sound of Hooves.* He has also written many successful plays, including *The Song of the Anvil* and *The Honey Spike* as well as the novel *Children of the Rainbow*. He has written *Jackomoora* and *Patsy-O* for children. He also translated the great classic *Peig* from Irish into English.

CLARE BOYLAN won the Benson and Hedges Award for outstanding work in journalism. Her first novel *Holy Picture* has been translated into many languages. Her short stories have appeared in *Best Irish Short Stories* and *Winter's Tale*. Her other published works include *A Nail on the Head* and *Last Resorts*. Her most recent novel *Black Baby* is now out in paperback and she has just published a new collection of short stories, *Concerning Virgins*.